ALL YOU NEED TO KNOW ABOUT NATIONAL PARK

NAME	ESTABLISHED AS PARK :	LOCATION
ACADIA	FEBRUARY 26, 1919	MAINE
AMERICAN SAMOA	OCTOBER 31, 1988	AMERICAN SAMOA
ARCHES	NOVEMBER 12, 1971	UTAH
BADLANDS	NOVEMBER 10, 1978	SOUTH DAKOTA
BIG BEND	JUNE 12, 1944	TEXAS
BISCAYNE	JUNE 28, 1980	FLORIDA

NAME	ESTABLISHED AS PARK :	LOCATION
BLANK CANYON OF THE GUNNISION	OCOTOBER 21, 1999	COLORADO
BRYCE CANYON	FEBRUARY 25, 1928	UTAH
CANYONLANDS	SEPTEMBER 12, 1964	UTAH
CAPITOL REEF	DECEMBER 18, 1971	UTAH
CARISBAD CAVERNS	MAY 14, 1930	NEW MEXICO
CHANNEL ISLANDS	MARCH 5,1980	CALIFORNIA

NAME	ESTABLISHED AS PARK :	LOCATION
CONGAREE	NOVEMBER 10, 2003	**SOUTH CAROLINA**
CRATER LAKE	MAY 22, 1902	**OREGON**
CUYAHOGA VALLEY	OCOTOBER 11, 2000	**OHIO**
DEATH VALLEY	OCTOBER 31, 1994	**CALIFORNIA**
DENALI	FEB 26, 1917	**ALASKA**
DRY TORTUGAS	OCOTBER 26, 1992	**FLORIDA**

NAME	ESTABLISHED AS PARK :	LOCATION
EVERGLADES	MAY 30, 1934	FLORIDA
GATES OF TGE ARCTIC	DECEMBER 2, 1980	ALASKA
GETWAY ARCH	FEBRUARY 22, 2018	MISSOURI
GLACIER BAY	DECEMBER 2, 1980	ALASKA
GLACIER	MAY 11, 1910	MONTANA
GRAND CANYON	FEB 26, 1919	ARIZONA

NAME	ESTABLISHED AS PARK :	LOCATION
GRAND TETON	FEB 26, 1929	WYOMING
GREAT BASIN	OCT 27, 1986	NEVADA
GREAT SAND DUNES	SEPT 13, 2004	COLORADO
GREAT SMOKY MOUNTAINS	JUNE 15, 1934	NORTH CAROLINA, TENNESSEE
GUADALUPE MOUNTAINS	OCT 15, 1966	TEXAS
HELEAKALA	JULY 1, 1961	HAWAII

NAME	ESTABLISHED AS PARK :	LOCATION
HAWAI'I VOLCANOES	AUG 1, 1916	**HAWAII**
HOT SPRINGS	MARCH 4, 1921	**ARKANSAS**
INDIANA DUNES	FEB 15, 2019	**INDIANA**
ISLE ROYAL	APRIL 3, 1940	**MICHIGAN**
JOSHUA TREE	OCT 31, 1994	**CALIFORNIA**
KATMAI	DECEMBER 2, 1980	**ALASKA**

NAME	ESTABLISHED AS PARK :	LOCATION
KENAI FJORDS	DEC 2, 1980	**ALASKA**
KINGS CANYON	MARCH 4, 1940	**CALIFORNIA**
KOBUK	DEC 2, 1980	**ALASKA**
LAKE CLARK	DEC 2, 1980	**ALASKA**
LASSEN VOLCANIC	AUG 9, 1916	**CALIFORNIA**
MAMMOTH CAVE	JULY 1, 1941	**KENTUCKY**

NAME	ESTABLISHED AS PARK :	LOCATION
MESA VERDE	JUNE 29, 1906	COLORADO
MOUNT RAINIER	MARCH 2, 1899	WASHINGTON
NEW RIVER GORGE	DEC 27, 2020	WEST VIRGINIA
NORTH CASCADES	OCTOBER 2, 1968	WASHINGTON
OLYMPIC	JUNE 29, 1938	WASHINGTON
PERTRIFIED FOREST	DEC 9, 1962	ARIZONA

NAME	ESTABLISHED AS PARK :	LOCATION
PINNACLES	JANUARY 10, 2013	CALIFORNIA
REDWOOD	OCTOBER 2, 1968	CALIFORNIA
ROCKY MOUNTAIN	JANUARY 26, 1915	COLORADO
SAGUARO	OCTOBER 14, 1994	ARIZONA
SEQUOIA	SEPTEMBER 25, 1890	CALIFORNIA
SHENANDOAH	DECEMBER 26, 1935	VIRGINIA

NAME	ESTABLISHED AS PARK :	LOCATION
THEODORE ROOSEVELT	NOV 10, 1978	**NORTH DAKOTA**
VIRGIN ISLANDS	AUG 2, 1956	**U. S. VIRGIN ISLANDS**
VOYAGEURS	APRIL, 1975	**MINNESOTA**
WHITE SANDS	DEC 20, 2019	**NEW MEXICO**
WIND CAVES	JANUARY 9, 1903	**SOUTH DAKOTA**
WRANGELL-ST. ELIAS	DEC 2, 1980	**ALASKA**

NAME	ESTABLISHED AS PARK :	LOCATION
YELLOWSTONE	MARCH 1, 1872	MONTANA IDAHO
YOSEMITE	OCTOBER 1, 1890	CALIFORNIA
ZION	NOV 19, 1919	UTAH

BUCKET LIST

	NAME	DATE
1		
2		
3		
4		
5		
6		
7		
8		
9		
10		
11		
12		
13		
14		
15		
16		
17		
18		
19		
20		

	NAME	DATE
21		
22		
23		
24		
25		
26		
27		
28		
29		
30		
31		
32		
33		
34		
35		
36		
37		
38		
39		
40		

	NAME	DATE
41		
42		
43		
44		
45		
46		
47		
48		
49		
50		
51		
52		
53		
54		
56		
57		
58		
59		
60		
61		

PARK #

DATE

NATIONAL PARK

LOCATION

LODGE

I WENT WITH

FEE

(. . . . .$)

MY FIRST IMPRESSION

WEATHER

DAYS

1 | 2 | 3 | 4 | +5

SIGHTS/HIKE/EXPERIENCES

WILDLIFE I SAW

FAVORITE MOMENTS

WILL I RETURN?

(YES / NO)

RATING

WHEN I LEFT, I FELT

PARK #

DATE

NATIONAL PARK

LOCATION

LODGE

I WENT WITH

FEE

(. . . . . $)

MY FIRST IMPRESSION

WEATHER

DAYS

1 | 2 | 3 | 4 | +5

SIGHTS/HIKE/EXPERIENCES

WILDLIFE I SAW

FAVORITE MOMENTS

WILL I RETURN?
(YES / NO)

RATING

10

WHEN I LEFT, I FELT

PARK #   DATE

NATIONAL PARK

LOCATION   LODGE

I WENT WITH   FEE

                                                (. . . . .$)

MY FIRST IMPRESSION

WEATHER   DAYS
      1 | 2 | 3 | 4 | +5

SIGHTS/HIKE/EXPERIENCES

WILDLIFE I SAW

FAVORITE MOMENTS

WILL I RETURN?   RATING

(YES / NO)   10

WHEN I LEFT, I FELT

PARK #   DATE

NATIONAL PARK

LOCATION   LODGE

I WENT WITH   FEE

                                              (. . . . . $)

MY FIRST IMPRESSION

WEATHER   DAYS

                          1 | 2 | 3 | 4 | +5

SIGHTS/HIKE/EXPERIENCES

WILDLIFE I SAW

FAVORITE MOMENTS

WILL I RETURN?   RATING

(YES / NO)

WHEN I LEFT, I FELT

PARK #   DATE

NATIONAL PARK

LOCATION   LODGE

I WENT WITH   FEE

                                            (. . . . . $)

MY FIRST IMPRESSION

WEATHER   DAYS
     1 | 2 | 3 | 4 | +5

SIGHTS/HIKE/EXPERIENCES

WILDLIFE I SAW

FAVORITE MOMENTS

WILL I RETURN?   RATING

(YES / NO)   10

WHEN I LEFT, I FELT

PARK #   DATE

NATIONAL PARK

LOCATION   LODGE

I WENT WITH   FEE

                                    (. . . . . $)

MY FIRST IMPRESSION

WEATHER   DAYS
   ❄
                                    1 | 2 | 3 | 4 | +5

SIGHTS/HIKE/EXPERIENCES

WILDLIFE I SAW

FAVORITE MOMENTS

WILL I RETURN?   RATING

(YES / NO)   10

WHEN I LEFT, I FELT

PARK #

DATE

NATIONAL PARK

LOCATION

LODGE

I WENT WITH

FEE

(. . . . . $)

MY FIRST IMPRESSION

WEATHER

DAYS

1 | 2 | 3 | 4 | + 5

SIGHTS/HIKE/EXPERIENCES

WILDLIFE I SAW

FAVORITE MOMENTS

WILL I RETURN?

RATING

(YES / NO)

10

WHEN I LEFT, I FELT

PARK #

DATE

NATIONAL PARK

LOCATION

LODGE

I WENT WITH

FEE

(. . . . . $)

MY FIRST IMPRESSION

WEATHER

DAYS

1 | 2 | 3 | 4 | +5

SIGHTS/HIKE/EXPERIENCES

WILDLIFE I SAW

FAVORITE MOMENTS

WILL I RETURN?

(YES / NO)

RATING

10

WHEN I LEFT, I FELT

PARK #   DATE

NATIONAL PARK

LOCATION   LODGE

I WENT WITH   FEE
                                                   (. . . . . $)

MY FIRST IMPRESSION

WEATHER   DAYS

                                1 | 2 | 3 | 4 | +5

SIGHTS/HIKE/EXPERIENCES

WILDLIFE I SAW

FAVORITE MOMENTS

WILL I RETURN?   RATING

(YES / NO)   10

WHEN I LEFT, I FELT

PARK #   DATE

NATIONAL PARK

LOCATION   LODGE

I WENT WITH   FEE

                                    (. . . . . $)

MY FIRST IMPRESSION

WEATHER   DAYS

                           1 | 2 | 3 | 4 | +5

SIGHTS/HIKE/EXPERIENCES

WILDLIFE I SAW

FAVORITE MOMENTS

WILL I RETURN?   RATING

(YES / NO)
                                    10

WHEN I LEFT, I FELT

PARK #   DATE

NATIONAL PARK

LOCATION   LODGE

I WENT WITH   FEE

                                   (. . . . . $)

MY FIRST IMPRESSION

WEATHER   DAYS

                     1 | 2 | 3 | 4 | +5

SIGHTS/HIKE/EXPERIENCES

WILDLIFE I SAW

FAVORITE MOMENTS

WILL I RETURN?   RATING

(YES / NO)   10

WHEN I LEFT, I FELT

PARK #   DATE

NATIONAL PARK

LOCATION   LODGE

I WENT WITH   FEE

                                                      (. . . . . $)

MY FIRST IMPRESSION

WEATHER   DAYS
              1 | 2 | 3 | 4 | +5

SIGHTS/HIKE/EXPERIENCES

WILDLIFE I SAW

FAVORITE MOMENTS

WILL I RETURN?   RATING

(YES / NO)
                                                10

WHEN I LEFT, I FELT

PARK #   DATE

NATIONAL PARK

LOCATION   LODGE

I WENT WITH   FEE

                                      (. . . . . $)

MY FIRST IMPRESSION

WEATHER   DAYS

                         1 | 2 | 3 | 4 | + 5

SIGHTS/HIKE/EXPERIENCES

WILDLIFE I SAW

FAVORITE MOMENTS

WILL I RETURN?   RATING

(YES / NO)

WHEN I LEFT, I FELT

PARK #   DATE

NATIONAL PARK

LOCATION   LODGE

I WENT WITH   FEE

                                            (. . . . . $)

MY FIRST IMPRESSION

WEATHER   DAYS

                                1 | 2 | 3 | 4 | +5

SIGHTS/HIKE/EXPERIENCES

WILDLIFE I SAW

FAVORITE MOMENTS

WILL I RETURN?   RATING

(YES / NO)   10

WHEN I LEFT, I FELT

PARK #   DATE

NATIONAL PARK

LOCATION   LODGE

I WENT WITH   FEE

                                (. . . . . $)

MY FIRST IMPRESSION

WEATHER   DAYS

   ❄   1 | 2 | 3 | 4 | +5

SIGHTS/HIKE/EXPERIENCES

WILDLIFE I SAW

FAVORITE MOMENTS

WILL I RETURN?   RATING

(YES / NO)   10

WHEN I LEFT, I FELT

PARK #   DATE

NATIONAL PARK

LOCATION   LODGE

I WENT WITH   FEE
                                (. . . . . $)

MY FIRST IMPRESSION

WEATHER   DAYS

                                1 | 2 | 3 | 4 | +5

SIGHTS/HIKE/EXPERIENCES

WILDLIFE I SAW

FAVORITE MOMENTS

WILL I RETURN?   RATING
(YES / NO)
                                10

WHEN I LEFT, I FELT

PARK #   DATE

NATIONAL PARK

LOCATION   LODGE

I WENT WITH   FEE

                                (. . . . .$)

MY FIRST IMPRESSION

WEATHER   DAYS

   ❄   1 | 2 | 3 | 4 | +5

SIGHTS/HIKE/EXPERIENCES

WILDLIFE I SAW

FAVORITE MOMENTS

WILL I RETURN?   RATING

(YES / NO)
                                                10

WHEN I LEFT, I FELT

PARK #

DATE

NATIONAL PARK

LOCATION

LODGE

I WENT WITH

FEE

(. . . . . $)

MY FIRST IMPRESSION

WEATHER

DAYS

1 | 2 | 3 | 4 | +5

SIGHTS/HIKE/EXPERIENCES

WILDLIFE I SAW

FAVORITE MOMENTS

WILL I RETURN?

RATING

(YES / NO)

10

WHEN I LEFT, I FELT

PARK #   DATE

NATIONAL PARK

LOCATION   LODGE

I WENT WITH   FEE

                                                 (. . . . . $)

MY FIRST IMPRESSION

WEATHER   DAYS
   ❄   1 | 2 | 3 | 4 | +5

SIGHTS/HIKE/EXPERIENCES

WILDLIFE I SAW

FAVORITE MOMENTS

WILL I RETURN?   RATING

(YES / NO)
                                                 | 10

WHEN I LEFT, I FELT

PARK #   DATE

NATIONAL PARK

LOCATION   LODGE

I WENT WITH   FEE

                                (. . . . . $)

MY FIRST IMPRESSION

WEATHER   DAYS

                                1 | 2 | 3 | 4 | +5

SIGHTS/HIKE/EXPERIENCES

WILDLIFE I SAW

FAVORITE MOMENTS

WILL I RETURN?   RATING

(YES / NO)   10

WHEN I LEFT, I FELT

PARK #   DATE

NATIONAL PARK

LOCATION   LODGE

I WENT WITH   FEE

                                      (. . . . . $)

MY FIRST IMPRESSION

WEATHER   DAYS
     1 | 2 | 3 | 4 | +5

SIGHTS/HIKE/EXPERIENCES

WILDLIFE I SAW

FAVORITE MOMENTS

WILL I RETURN?   RATING

(YES / NO)   10

WHEN I LEFT, I FELT

PARK #   **DATE**

NATIONAL PARK

LOCATION   **LODGE**

I WENT WITH   **FEE**

(. . . . . $)

MY FIRST IMPRESSION

WEATHER   **DAYS**

1 | 2 | 3 | 4 | +5

SIGHTS/HIKE/EXPERIENCES

WILDLIFE I SAW

FAVORITE MOMENTS

WILL I RETURN?   **RATING**

(YES / NO)

WHEN I LEFT, I FELT

PARK #   DATE

NATIONAL PARK

LOCATION   LODGE

I WENT WITH   FEE

                                    (. . . . . $)

MY FIRST IMPRESSION

WEATHER   DAYS

   ❄   1 | 2 | 3 | 4 | +5

SIGHTS/HIKE/EXPERIENCES

WILDLIFE I SAW

FAVORITE MOMENTS

WILL I RETURN?   RATING

(YES / NO)
                                            10

WHEN I LEFT, I FELT

PARK #   **DATE**

NATIONAL PARK

LOCATION   **LODGE**

I WENT WITH   **FEE**

                                                  (. . . . . $)

MY FIRST IMPRESSION

WEATHER   **DAYS**

                              1 | 2 | 3 | 4 | +5

SIGHTS/HIKE/EXPERIENCES

WILDLIFE I SAW

FAVORITE MOMENTS

WILL I RETURN?   **RATING**

(YES / NO)   10

WHEN I LEFT, I FELT

PARK #

DATE

NATIONAL PARK

LOCATION

LODGE

I WENT WITH

FEE

(. . . . . $)

MY FIRST IMPRESSION

WEATHER

DAYS

1 | 2 | 3 | 4 | + 5

SIGHTS/HIKE/EXPERIENCES

WILDLIFE I SAW

FAVORITE MOMENTS

WILL I RETURN?

RATING

(YES / NO)

10

WHEN I LEFT, I FELT

PARK #   DATE

NATIONAL PARK

LOCATION   LODGE

I WENT WITH   FEE

                                      (. . . . . $)

MY FIRST IMPRESSION

WEATHER   DAYS

                           1 | 2 | 3 | 4 | + 5

SIGHTS/HIKE/EXPERIENCES

WILDLIFE I SAW

FAVORITE MOMENTS

WILL I RETURN?   RATING
(YES / NO)

WHEN I LEFT, I FELT

PARK #   DATE

NATIONAL PARK

LOCATION   LODGE

I WENT WITH   FEE

                                    (. . . . . $)

MY FIRST IMPRESSION

WEATHER   DAYS

      1 | 2 | 3 | 4 | +5

SIGHTS/HIKE/EXPERIENCES

WILDLIFE I SAW

FAVORITE MOMENTS

WILL I RETURN?   RATING

(YES / NO)
                                    10

WHEN I LEFT, I FELT

PARK #   DATE

NATIONAL PARK

LOCATION   LODGE

I WENT WITH   FEE

                                                (. . . . . $)

MY FIRST IMPRESSION

WEATHER   DAYS

                                1 | 2 | 3 | 4 | +5

SIGHTS/HIKE/EXPERIENCES

WILDLIFE I SAW

FAVORITE MOMENTS

WILL I RETURN?   RATING

(YES / NO)   10

WHEN I LEFT, I FELT

PARK # DATE

NATIONAL PARK

LOCATION LODGE

I WENT WITH FEE

(. . . . .$)

MY FIRST IMPRESSION

WEATHER DAYS

1 | 2 | 3 | 4 | + 5

SIGHTS/HIKE/EXPERIENCES

WILDLIFE I SAW

FAVORITE MOMENTS

WILL I RETURN? RATING

(YES / NO) 10

WHEN I LEFT, I FELT

PARK #   DATE

NATIONAL PARK

LOCATION   LODGE

I WENT WITH   FEE

                                            (. . . . . $)

MY FIRST IMPRESSION

WEATHER   DAYS
     1 | 2 | 3 | 4 | +5

SIGHTS/HIKE/EXPERIENCES

WILDLIFE I SAW

FAVORITE MOMENTS

WILL I RETURN?   RATING

(YES / NO)   10

WHEN I LEFT, I FELT

PARK #   DATE

NATIONAL PARK

LOCATION   LODGE

I WENT WITH   FEE

                                     (. . . . . $)

MY FIRST IMPRESSION

WEATHER   DAYS

                          1 | 2 | 3 | 4 | + 5

SIGHTS/HIKE/EXPERIENCES

WILDLIFE I SAW

FAVORITE MOMENTS

WILL I RETURN?   RATING

(YES / NO)   10

WHEN I LEFT, I FELT

PARK #   DATE

NATIONAL PARK

LOCATION   LODGE

I WENT WITH   FEE

                                      (. . . . . $)

MY FIRST IMPRESSION

WEATHER   DAYS

                          1 | 2 | 3 | 4 | +5

SIGHTS/HIKE/EXPERIENCES

WILDLIFE I SAW

FAVORITE MOMENTS

WILL I RETURN?   RATING

(YES / NO)
                                      10

WHEN I LEFT, I FELT

PARK #   DATE

NATIONAL PARK

LOCATION   LODGE

I WENT WITH   FEE

                                      (. . . . .$)

MY FIRST IMPRESSION

WEATHER   DAYS

                             1 | 2 | 3 | 4 | +5

SIGHTS/HIKE/EXPERIENCES

WILDLIFE I SAW

FAVORITE MOMENTS

WILL I RETURN?   RATING

(YES / NO)   10

WHEN I LEFT, I FELT

PARK #   DATE

NATIONAL PARK

LOCATION   LODGE

I WENT WITH   FEE

                                (. . . . . $)

MY FIRST IMPRESSION

WEATHER   DAYS
     1 | 2 | 3 | 4 | +5

SIGHTS/HIKE/EXPERIENCES

WILDLIFE I SAW

FAVORITE MOMENTS

WILL I RETURN?   RATING

(YES / NO)
                                    10

WHEN I LEFT, I FELT

PARK #

DATE

NATIONAL PARK

LOCATION

LODGE

I WENT WITH

FEE

(. . . . . $)

MY FIRST IMPRESSION

WEATHER

DAYS

1 | 2 | 3 | 4 | +5

SIGHTS/HIKE/EXPERIENCES

WILDLIFE I SAW

FAVORITE MOMENTS

WILL I RETURN?

RATING

(YES / NO)

10

WHEN I LEFT, I FELT

PARK #   DATE

NATIONAL PARK

LOCATION   LODGE

I WENT WITH   FEE
                                                (. . . . . $)

MY FIRST IMPRESSION

WEATHER   DAYS
        1 | 2 | 3 | 4 | +5

SIGHTS/HIKE/EXPERIENCES

WILDLIFE I SAW

FAVORITE MOMENTS

WILL I RETURN?   RATING

(YES / NO)   10

WHEN I LEFT, I FELT

PARK #   **DATE**

NATIONAL PARK

LOCATION   **LODGE**

I WENT WITH   **FEE**

                                                (. . . . . $)

MY FIRST IMPRESSION

WEATHER   **DAYS**

                              1 | 2 | 3 | 4 | + 5

SIGHTS/HIKE/EXPERIENCES

WILDLIFE I SAW

FAVORITE MOMENTS

WILL I RETURN?   **RATING**

(YES / NO)

10

WHEN I LEFT, I FELT

PARK #   DATE

NATIONAL PARK

LOCATION   LODGE

I WENT WITH   FEE

                                    (. . . . . $)

MY FIRST IMPRESSION

WEATHER   DAYS
       1 | 2 | 3 | 4 | +5

SIGHTS/HIKE/EXPERIENCES

WILDLIFE I SAW

FAVORITE MOMENTS

WILL I RETURN?   RATING

(YES / NO)   10

WHEN I LEFT, I FELT

PARK #   DATE

NATIONAL PARK

LOCATION   LODGE

I WENT WITH   FEE

                                (. . . . . $)

MY FIRST IMPRESSION

WEATHER   DAYS

   ❄   1 | 2 | 3 | 4 | +5

SIGHTS / HIKE / EXPERIENCES

WILDLIFE I SAW

FAVORITE MOMENTS

WILL I RETURN?   RATING

(YES / NO)
                                           10

WHEN I LEFT, I FELT

PARK #   DATE

NATIONAL PARK

LOCATION   LODGE

I WENT WITH   FEE

                                          (. . . . . $)

MY FIRST IMPRESSION

WEATHER   DAYS

                          1 | 2 | 3 | 4 | +5

SIGHTS/HIKE/EXPERIENCES

WILDLIFE I SAW

FAVORITE MOMENTS

WILL I RETURN?   RATING

(YES / NO)   10

WHEN I LEFT, I FELT

PARK #   DATE

NATIONAL PARK

LOCATION   LODGE

I WENT WITH   FEE

                                    (. . . . .$)

MY FIRST IMPRESSION

WEATHER   DAYS

   ❄   1 | 2 | 3 | 4 | +5

SIGHTS/HIKE/EXPERIENCES

WILDLIFE I SAW

FAVORITE MOMENTS

WILL I RETURN?   RATING

(YES / NO)
                                              10

WHEN I LEFT, I FELT

PARK #   DATE

NATIONAL PARK

LOCATION   LODGE

I WENT WITH   FEE

                                (. . . . . $)

MY FIRST IMPRESSION

WEATHER   DAYS

   ❄   1 | 2 | 3 | 4 | +5

SIGHTS/HIKE/EXPERIENCES

WILDLIFE I SAW

FAVORITE MOMENTS

WILL I RETURN?   RATING

(YES / NO)
                                                10

WHEN I LEFT, I FELT

PARK #

DATE

NATIONAL PARK

LOCATION

LODGE

I WENT WITH

FEE

(. . . . .$)

MY FIRST IMPRESSION

WEATHER

DAYS

1 | 2 | 3 | 4 | + 5

SIGHTS/HIKE/EXPERIENCES

WILDLIFE I SAW

FAVORITE MOMENTS

WILL I RETURN?

RATING

(YES / NO)

WHEN I LEFT, I FELT

PARK # DATE

NATIONAL PARK

LOCATION LODGE

I WENT WITH FEE

(. . . . . $)

MY FIRST IMPRESSION

WEATHER DAYS

1 | 2 | 3 | 4 | +5

SIGHTS/HIKE/EXPERIENCES

WILDLIFE I SAW

FAVORITE MOMENTS

WILL I RETURN? RATING

(YES / NO) 10

WHEN I LEFT, I FELT

PARK #   DATE

NATIONAL PARK

LOCATION   LODGE

I WENT WITH   FEE

                                        (. . . . . $)

MY FIRST IMPRESSION

WEATHER   DAYS
   1 | 2 | 3 | 4 | +5

SIGHTS/HIKE/EXPERIENCES

WILDLIFE I SAW

FAVORITE MOMENTS

WILL I RETURN?   RATING

(YES / NO)   10

WHEN I LEFT, I FELT

PARK #

DATE

NATIONAL PARK

LOCATION

LODGE

I WENT WITH

FEE

(. . . . . $)

MY FIRST IMPRESSION

WEATHER

DAYS

1 | 2 | 3 | 4 | +5

SIGHTS/HIKE/EXPERIENCES

WILDLIFE I SAW

FAVORITE MOMENTS

WILL I RETURN?

RATING

(YES / NO)

10

WHEN I LEFT, I FELT

PARK #   DATE

NATIONAL PARK

LOCATION   LODGE

I WENT WITH   FEE

                                      (. . . . . $)

MY FIRST IMPRESSION

WEATHER   DAYS

   1 | 2 | 3 | 4 | +5

SIGHTS / HIKE / EXPERIENCES

WILDLIFE I SAW

FAVORITE MOMENTS

WILL I RETURN?   RATING

(YES / NO)   10

WHEN I LEFT, I FELT

PARK #

DATE

NATIONAL PARK

LOCATION

LODGE

I WENT WITH

FEE

(. . . . .$)

MY FIRST IMPRESSION

WEATHER

DAYS

1 | 2 | 3 | 4 | + 5

SIGHTS / HIKE / EXPERIENCES

WILDLIFE I SAW

FAVORITE MOMENTS

WILL I RETURN?

RATING

(YES / NO)

10

WHEN I LEFT, I FELT

PARK #   DATE

NATIONAL PARK

LOCATION   LODGE

I WENT WITH   FEE

                                    (. . . . . $)

MY FIRST IMPRESSION

WEATHER   DAYS

                                    1 | 2 | 3 | 4 | +5

SIGHTS/HIKE/EXPERIENCES

WILDLIFE I SAW

FAVORITE MOMENTS

WILL I RETURN?   RATING

(YES / NO)   10

WHEN I LEFT, I FELT

PARK #   DATE

NATIONAL PARK

LOCATION   LODGE

I WENT WITH   FEE

                                         (. . . . . $)

MY FIRST IMPRESSION

WEATHER   DAYS

   ❄   1 | 2 | 3 | 4 | +5

SIGHTS/HIKE/EXPERIENCES

WILDLIFE I SAW

FAVORITE MOMENTS

WILL I RETURN?   RATING

(YES / NO)
                                                    10

WHEN I LEFT, I FELT

PARK #   DATE

NATIONAL PARK

LOCATION   LODGE

I WENT WITH   FEE

                                                   (. . . . . $)

MY FIRST IMPRESSION

WEATHER   DAYS
           1 | 2 | 3 | 4 | +5

SIGHTS/HIKE/EXPERIENCES

WILDLIFE I SAW

FAVORITE MOMENTS

WILL I RETURN?   RATING

(YES / NO)   10

WHEN I LEFT, I FELT

PARK #   DATE

NATIONAL PARK

LOCATION   LODGE

I WENT WITH   FEE

                                    (. . . . .$)

MY FIRST IMPRESSION

WEATHER   DAYS
     1 | 2 | 3 | 4 | +5

SIGHTS/HIKE/EXPERIENCES

WILDLIFE I SAW

FAVORITE MOMENTS

WILL I RETURN?   RATING

(YES / NO)
                                              10

WHEN I LEFT, I FELT

PARK #

DATE

NATIONAL PARK

LOCATION

LODGE

I WENT WITH

FEE

(. . . . .$)

MY FIRST IMPRESSION

WEATHER

DAYS

1 | 2 | 3 | 4 | +5

SIGHTS/HIKE/EXPERIENCES

WILDLIFE I SAW

FAVORITE MOMENTS

WILL I RETURN?

(YES / NO)

RATING

10

WHEN I LEFT, I FELT

PARK # DATE

NATIONAL PARK

LOCATION LODGE

I WENT WITH FEE

(. . . . . $)

MY FIRST IMPRESSION

WEATHER DAYS

  1 | 2 | 3 | 4 | +5

SIGHTS/HIKE/EXPERIENCES

WILDLIFE I SAW

FAVORITE MOMENTS

WILL I RETURN? RATING

(YES / NO) 10

WHEN I LEFT, I FELT

PARK #

DATE

NATIONAL PARK

LOCATION

LODGE

I WENT WITH

FEE

(. . . . .$)

MY FIRST IMPRESSION

WEATHER

DAYS

1 | 2 | 3 | 4 | +5

SIGHTS/HIKE/EXPERIENCES

WILDLIFE I SAW

FAVORITE MOMENTS

WILL I RETURN?

RATING

(YES / NO)

10

WHEN I LEFT, I FELT

PARK #   DATE

NATIONAL PARK

LOCATION   LODGE

I WENT WITH   FEE
                                (. . . . .$)

MY FIRST IMPRESSION

WEATHER   DAYS

                                1 | 2 | 3 | 4 | +5

SIGHTS/HIKE/EXPERIENCES

WILDLIFE I SAW

FAVORITE MOMENTS

WILL I RETURN?   RATING
(YES / NO)
                                        10

WHEN I LEFT, I FELT

PARK #   DATE

NATIONAL PARK

LOCATION   LODGE

I WENT WITH   FEE

                                            (. . . . . $)

MY FIRST IMPRESSION

WEATHER   DAYS

   1 | 2 | 3 | 4 | +5

SIGHTS/HIKE/EXPERIENCES

WILDLIFE I SAW

FAVORITE MOMENTS

WILL I RETURN?   RATING

(YES / NO)
                                            10

WHEN I LEFT, I FELT

PARK #

DATE

NATIONAL PARK

LOCATION

LODGE

I WENT WITH

FEE

(. . . . .$)

MY FIRST IMPRESSION

WEATHER

DAYS

1 | 2 | 3 | 4 | + 5

SIGHTS/HIKE/EXPERIENCES

WILDLIFE I SAW

FAVORITE MOMENTS

WILL I RETURN?

(YES / NO)

RATING

10

WHEN I LEFT, I FELT

PARK #   DATE

NATIONAL PARK

LOCATION   LODGE

I WENT WITH   FEE
                                            (. . . . . $)

MY FIRST IMPRESSION

WEATHER   DAYS
    1 | 2 | 3 | 4 | +5

SIGHTS/HIKE/EXPERIENCES

WILDLIFE I SAW

FAVORITE MOMENTS

WILL I RETURN?   RATING
(YES / NO)
                                            10

WHEN I LEFT, I FELT

PARK #

DATE

NATIONAL PARK

LOCATION

LODGE

I WENT WITH

FEE

(. . . . .$)

MY FIRST IMPRESSION

WEATHER

DAYS

1 | 2 | 3 | 4 | + 5

SIGHTS/HIKE/EXPERIENCES

WILDLIFE I SAW

FAVORITE MOMENTS

WILL I RETURN?

(YES / NO)

RATING

10

WHEN I LEFT, I FELT

PARK #   DATE

NATIONAL PARK

LOCATION   LODGE

I WENT WITH   FEE

                                    (. . . . . $)

MY FIRST IMPRESSION

WEATHER   DAYS

☀ ☁   1 | 2 | 3 | 4 | +5

SIGHTS/HIKE/EXPERIENCES

WILDLIFE I SAW

FAVORITE MOMENTS

WILL I RETURN?   RATING

(YES / NO)
                                    10

WHEN I LEFT, I FELT

PARK #

DATE

NATIONAL PARK

LOCATION

LODGE

I WENT WITH

FEE

(. . . . . $)

MY FIRST IMPRESSION

WEATHER

DAYS

1 | 2 | 3 | 4 | + 5

SIGHTS / HIKE / EXPERIENCES

WILDLIFE I SAW

FAVORITE MOMENTS

WILL I RETURN?

(YES / NO)

RATING

10

WHEN I LEFT, I FELT

IF YOU ENJOY THIS BOOK, A QUICK REVIEW ON OUR AMAZON BOOK PAGE WOULD REALLY HELP.

THANK YOU.

Made in the USA
Middletown, DE
29 March 2022